Brea...

Written by
Claire Llewellyn

Contents

Collins

Day in, day out

There's something you do every day of your life, no matter where you are or what you're doing: it's breathing.

You breathe in and out every few seconds of the day and night. You couldn't stop breathing if you tried.

When you breathe, you take in air. Air is very important because it contains **oxygen**, a **gas** you need to survive. Oxygen is important for all life – animals need it too.

All about oxygen

Oxygen is invisible, but it's all
around you ... it's in the air
... it's in water too.

Oxygen has no colour,
taste or smell,
but you can't live
without it.

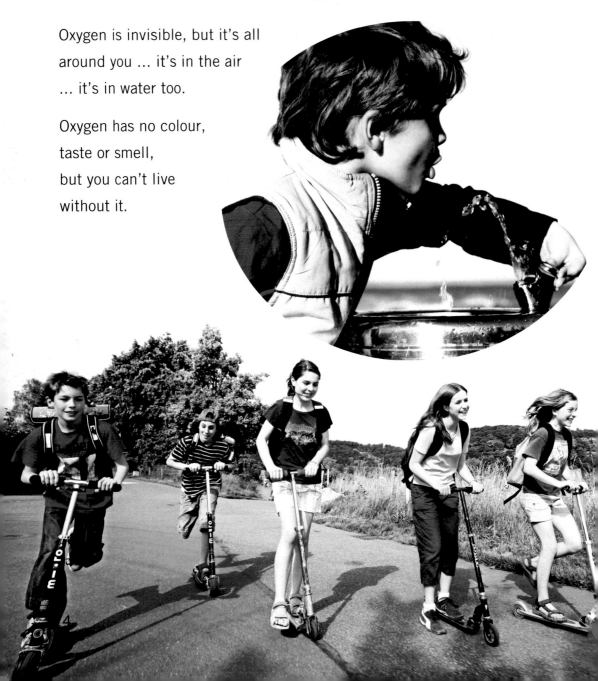

Oxygen works inside your body. It helps to release the **energy** in your food. Every **cell** in your body needs energy to work. This is what keeps you moving, working, thinking and growing. This is what keeps you alive!

Your body can't store oxygen. You need to breathe it all the time, and you have two special **organs** that do this for you. They're called lungs.

Lungs or gills?

Every animal that lives on land has lungs
to breathe in air. Your lungs lie inside
your chest. They're like spongy balloons
that stretch and fill with air.

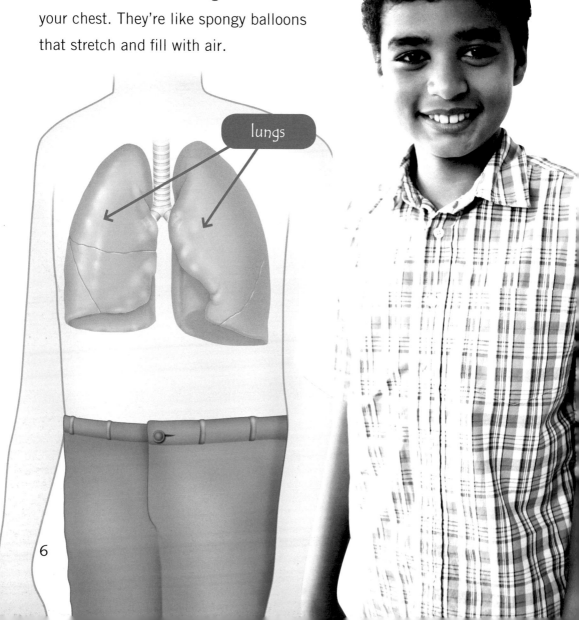

lungs

Fish and other animals that live in water take in oxygen a different way. They have gills instead of lungs. A fish has two sets of gills, one on each side of its head. The gills look very red because they're full of blood. As a fish swims along, it gulps down water through its mouth. When the water flows over its gills, oxygen passes into its blood.

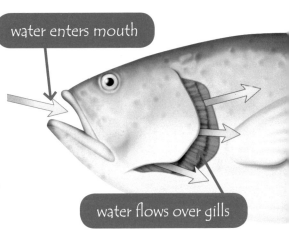

water enters mouth

water flows over gills

Did you know?

Some sea animals do have lungs. Turtles, whales, dolphins and seals hold their breath when they dive under water, and then come back to the surface for air.

Inside your chest

Touch your chest with your fingers and you'll feel a hard, bony cage. It's made of pairs of ribs, which protect your soft lungs. Your ribcage also protects your heart, which lies between your lungs.

Under your ribs is a strong sheet of **muscle** in the shape of a dome. This muscle helps you to breathe. When it **contracts**, it flattens down so the space inside your chest gets larger. Your lungs **expand** into the space and suck air into your body.

Breathing in

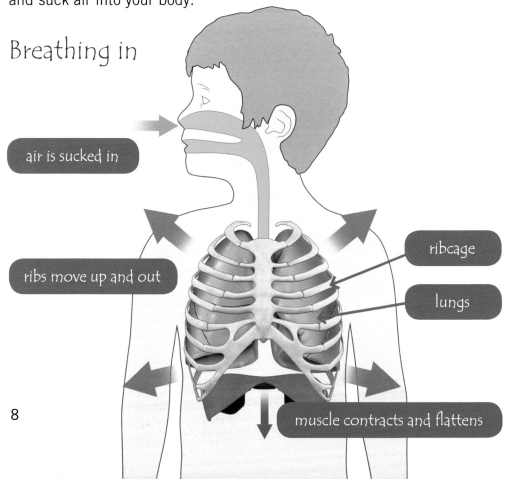

air is sucked in

ribs move up and out

ribcage

lungs

muscle contracts and flattens

When you breathe out, the muscle under your ribs relaxes and returns to the shape of a dome. This makes your chest smaller and pushes air out of your lungs.

There are also muscles between your ribs. When they contract, they lift your ribs so your lungs have room to fill. When you breathe out, the muscles relax and your ribs lower again.

Try it out!

Put your hands on your chest and breathe in deeply. You will feel your chest getting bigger as your lungs fill with air. Now breathe out the air. You will feel your chest go back to its usual size.

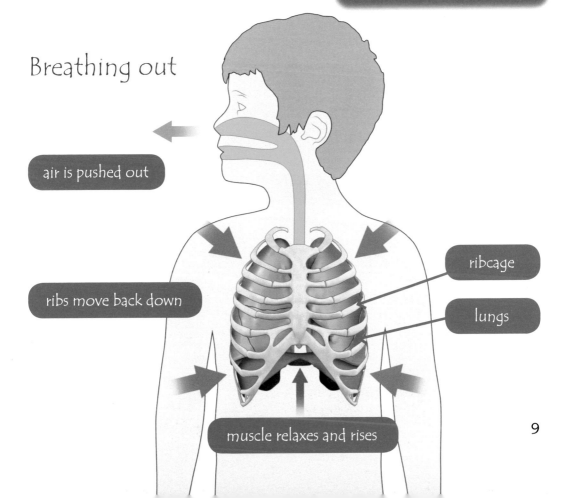

Breathing out

air is pushed out

ribs move back down

ribcage

lungs

muscle relaxes and rises

9

Into your nose

Each time you breathe in, air enters the nostrils in your nose. It moves along tubes called **airways**, which carry air in and out of your body. Your nostrils are lined with hairs and sticky **mucus**, which trap specks of dust and keep the airways clean. Your nostrils also warm your breath to protect your lungs from the cold.

Your breath flows down the back of your throat and into a tube called the windpipe. This carries air to and from your lungs and is the biggest airway in your body. It has strong walls that won't cave in and a sticky lining to trap dirt. At the bottom, your windpipe forks into two: one tube leads into your left lung; the other leads into your right.

Did you know?

Food sometimes goes down the wrong way and gets into your windpipe. This could block the airway and stop air getting to your lungs, so your brain orders you to cough and sneeze until you get the food out.

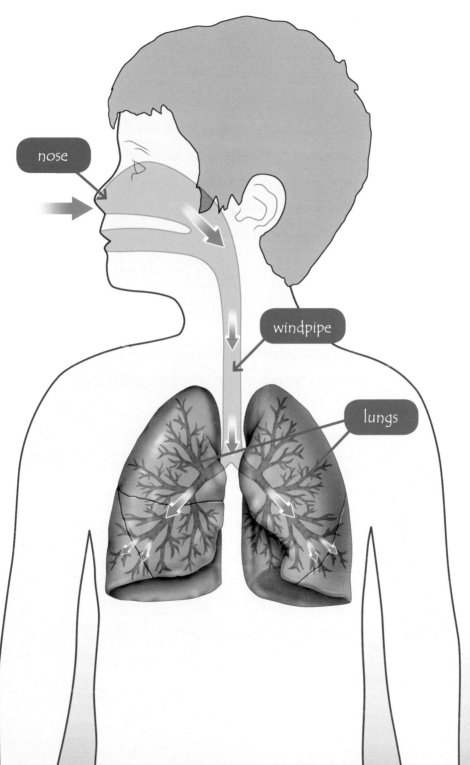

nose

windpipe

lungs

Into your lungs

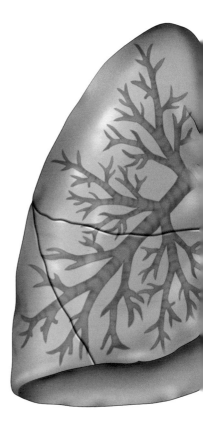

Your breath leaves your windpipe and enters your lungs. Inside, there are a lot more airways. Each one branches many times into smaller and smaller tubes, just like the branches on a tree. The smallest airways are finer than hairs and end in a tiny, bubbly air bag. The walls of the bag are thin and **moist**. They are covered in **microscopic** blood **vessels**; their walls are thin too.

Your breath fills all the airways. When it reaches the bubbly air bags, oxygen mixes with the moisture. This seeps through the air bag, into the blood vessels and enters your blood. Now it flows to your heart.

Did you know?

There are about 700 million tiny air bags inside your lungs. If you could spread them out, they'd cover a tennis court! This big surface allows a lot of oxygen to enter your blood.

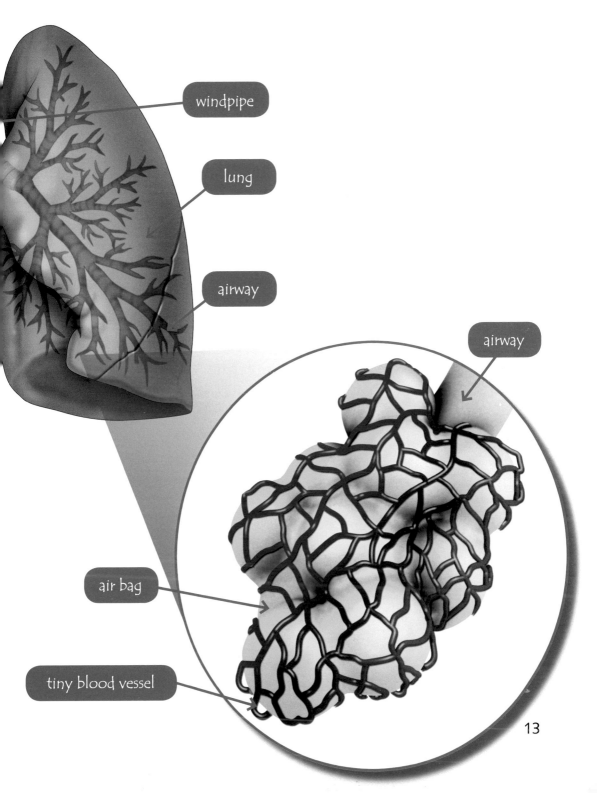

windpipe

lung

airway

airway

air bag

tiny blood vessel

13

On to your heart

Your heart is a powerful **pump** that beats all the time. Before each beat, the left side of your heart fills up with blood from your lungs. Then the muscles in your heart contract, and squeeze the blood out. It flows along the blood vessels in your body until every organ, muscle and cell gets the oxygen it needs.

As the cells in your body use oxygen, they make a waste gas called **carbon dioxide**. Too much of this gas is bad for your body so you need to breathe it out. Your blood picks it up and carries it back to your heart and lungs.

Did you know?

The blood that flows out from your heart is bright red because it contains fresh oxygen. The blood that flows back to your heart is a much darker red because a lot of the oxygen has been used up.

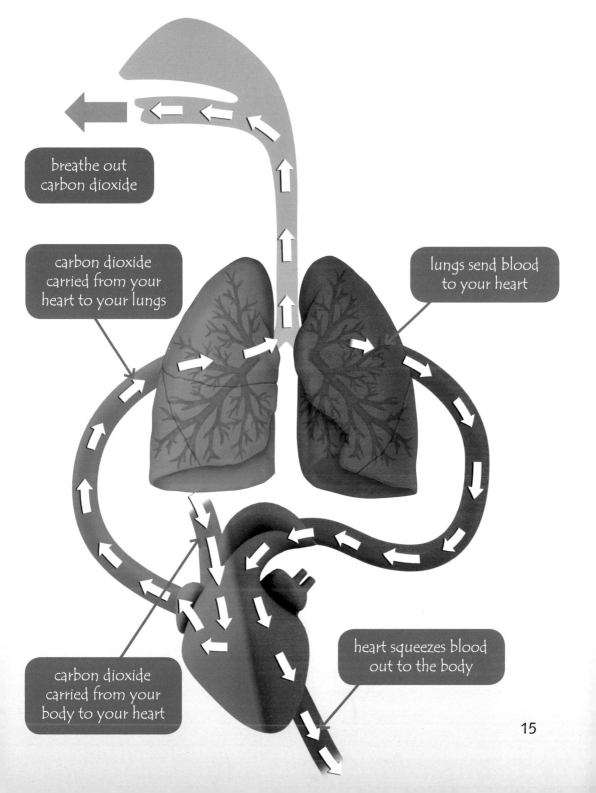

breathe out carbon dioxide

carbon dioxide carried from your heart to your lungs

lungs send blood to your heart

carbon dioxide carried from your body to your heart

heart squeezes blood out to the body

Breathing out

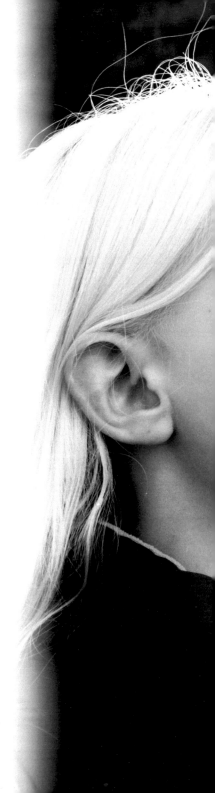

The blood from your body enters the right side of your heart. As the muscles in your heart contract, the blood is pumped back to your lungs. Here, the carbon dioxide seeps out and passes into the bubbly air bags inside your lungs. As you breathe out, the gas leaves your lungs: it flows back along the airways, up your windpipe and out through your nose.

The air you breathe out is warmer and wetter than the air you breathe in. This is because your body is warm and your lungs are moist. You can see the moisture in your breath when you breathe on to cool glass or into the air on a cold day.

Did you know?

It takes about one minute for your body to breathe in, deliver oxygen to your cells, pick up their waste gas, carry it to your lungs and breathe it out.

Try it out!

Put your hand in front of your mouth and breathe out. How does the air feel on the palm of your hand?

Work those lungs!

When you're running fast, your muscles are working hard. They need more oxygen to keep going and so you puff and breathe more deeply. You breathe through your mouth as well as your nose to take in extra air. At the same time, your heart beats faster. It's delivering oxygen-rich blood to your muscles as quickly as it can.

Puffing and panting is good for you! Exercise helps your lungs grow stronger so they supply more oxygen to the body. It's important to be active every day. Running, dancing, skipping and swimming are much better for you than sitting still, and will strengthen your lungs.

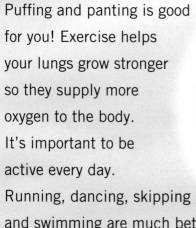

Did you know?

Playing some musical instruments, such as the mouth organ, trumpet or recorder, helps to make your lungs stronger.

The brain and breathing

When you swim and dive underwater, you have to hold your breath. It's impossible to do this for long: your brain drives you up to the surface to fill your lungs with air.

Your brain is always in control of your breathing. It knows how much oxygen you have in your blood. If you're active and using a lot of oxygen, your brain orders your chest muscles to work harder and breathe in more. If you're asleep and using very little oxygen, your brain orders your muscles to work more slowly.

Your brain itself needs oxygen to work. If your brain runs out of oxygen, it stops working properly. This is very dangerous: after just five minutes without oxygen, brain cells begin to die.

An adult's breathing rate

Action	Breaths per minute
Sleeping	12–15
Normal breathing	12–20
After exercise	40

Did you know?

An adult's lungs hold about five litres of air. A tall person's lungs hold more than a shorter person's. A man's lungs hold more than a woman's.

Talking and breathing

Your breath helps you to talk and sing. It works with an organ called the voice box, which lies inside your throat. Your voice box contains two stringy cords. When you want to make a sound, you breathe air out of your lungs while muscles in your voice box pull on the cords. As the air passes between them, the cords shake and make a sound. This moves up to your mouth and you use your tongue, cheeks, lips and teeth to turn it into speech.

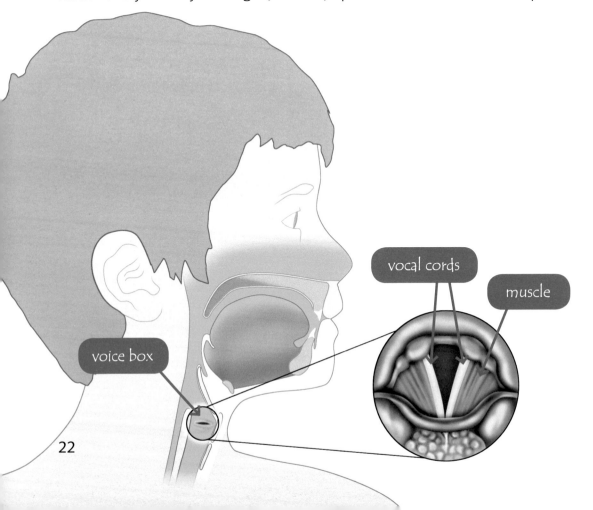

vocal cords

muscle

voice box

The more air you blow out from your lungs, the louder and longer a sound will be. Shouting takes a lot of air so if you want to shout a lot you'll need to breathe in plenty.

Did you know?
A belly laugh uses one long breath, but when you giggle you let out your breath a little at a time.

Breathing problems

Some people have a problem breathing because they have a disease called asthma. If you have asthma, the airways inside your lungs are always red and sore. Smoke, dust or other things can irritate these tiny airways and make them tighten. This makes it hard to breathe in and out.

People can control their asthma with medicine, which comes in a pack called a puffer. They suck the medicine into their lungs. It quickly opens the airways and makes it easier to breathe.

Other things, such as air **pollution**, can also make breathing difficult. Cars and trucks pollute the air in cities and on busy roads. Polluted air can irritate the lungs and make people cough or feel short of breath. It can also bring on asthma attacks.

Did you know?
Many things can start an asthma attack: pets, windy weather as well as colds and flu.

Lungs hate smoke

Smoking damages the lungs. The smoke from cigarettes contains tiny specks of brown, sticky tar and many dangerous gases. These damage the airways in the body and, in time, can cause disease. The airways also work less well: they allow more dirt into the lungs. This produces a lot of mucus, which causes a nasty cough.

lung from a non-smoker

lung from a smoker

Did you know?
Smoking stains the lungs black. Healthy lungs are pink.

The gases in the smoke move from the lungs and enter the blood. They travel to every organ in the body, where they can cause health problems, such as heart disease. Smoking also makes the blood vessels narrow so less oxygen-rich blood is delivered to the muscles. Smokers have less energy: when they are active, their muscles hurt and they soon feel tired.

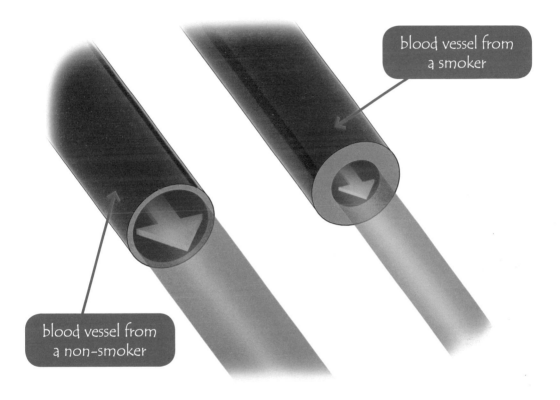

blood vessel from a smoker

blood vessel from a non-smoker

You don't have to smoke cigarettes to suffer damage in this way. Breathing someone else's smoke is almost as harmful for your lungs, especially if you have asthma.

Glossary

airways   passages for air to travel from the nose or mouth to the lungs

carbon dioxide   an invisible gas which is in the air – plants and animals need it to live

cell   one of the tiny pieces that are the basic building blocks of living things

contracts   becomes smaller

energy   the power to be active

expand   become larger

gas   something that can take any shape, and isn't a solid or a liquid

microscopic   so small that it can only be seen under a microscope

moist   a bit wet

mucus   the slimy stuff that's made inside your nose

muscle   something in your body that helps to make it move

organs   parts of a person or animal made up of cells which do a special job in the body, like the liver, kidney or heart

oxygen   a gas without any colour, taste or smell, which we breathe to stay alive

pollution   spoiling the earth with harmful rubbish

pump   something that pushes liquids through the body

vessels   tubes, like veins or arteries, which carry blood around the body

Index

How you breathe

Breathing in

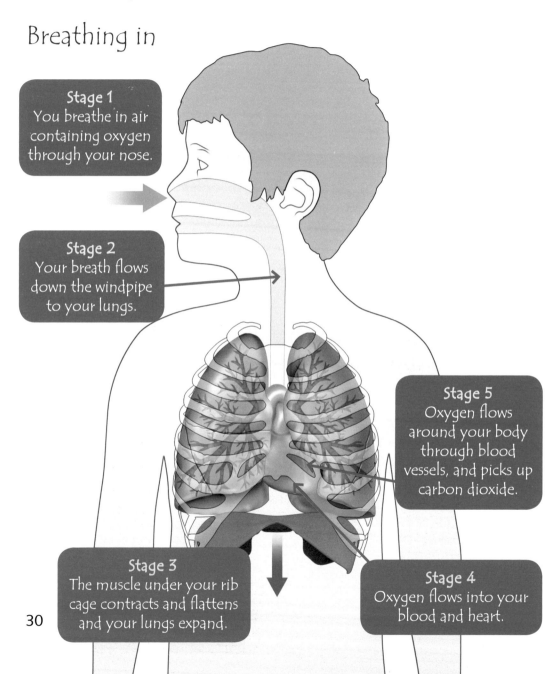

Stage 1
You breathe in air containing oxygen through your nose.

Stage 2
Your breath flows down the windpipe to your lungs.

Stage 5
Oxygen flows around your body through blood vessels, and picks up carbon dioxide.

Stage 3
The muscle under your rib cage contracts and flattens and your lungs expand.

Stage 4
Oxygen flows into your blood and heart.

Breathing out

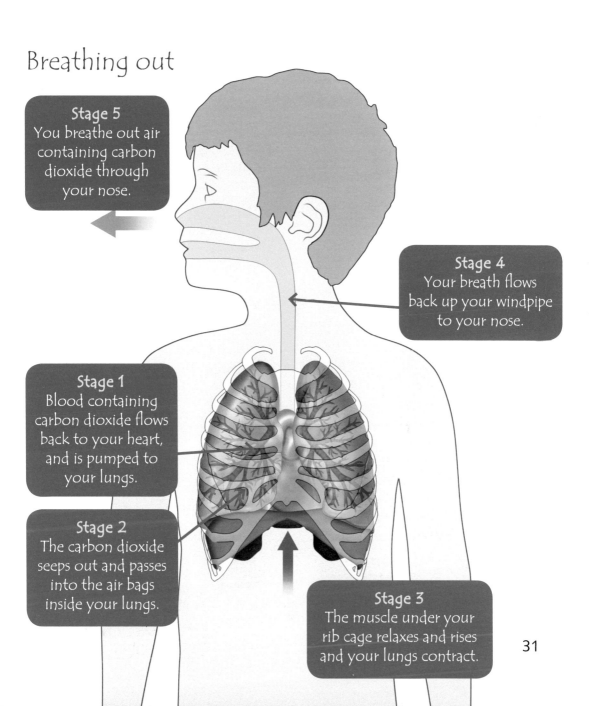

Stage 5
You breathe out air containing carbon dioxide through your nose.

Stage 4
Your breath flows back up your windpipe to your nose.

Stage 1
Blood containing carbon dioxide flows back to your heart, and is pumped to your lungs.

Stage 2
The carbon dioxide seeps out and passes into the air bags inside your lungs.

Stage 3
The muscle under your rib cage relaxes and rises and your lungs contract.

Ideas for reading

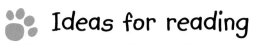

Written by Linda Pagett B.Ed (hons), M.Ed
Lecturer and Educational Consultant

Learning objectives: identify and make notes of the main sections of text; identify how different texts are organised; spell unfamiliar words using morphological rules; select and use a range of technical and descriptive vocabulary; use talk to organise roles and action; use some drama strategies to explore issues

Curriculum links: Science

Interest words: airways, carbon, dioxide, cell, contracts, energy, expand, gas, microscopic, moist, mucus, muscle, organs, oxygen, pollution, pump, vessels

Resources: whiteboard, paper, pens

Getting started

This book can be read over two or more reading sessions.

- Invite children to breathe in and hold their breath for 30 seconds. Ask them to observe what has happened, e.g. chest rising, and speculate what has changed inside their body, making notes on the whiteboard.

- Invite one of the children to read the blurb on the cover and discuss in what ways we can use our breath, e.g. blowing out matches, blowing up balloons.

- Discuss what can help you read information books, e.g. previous knowledge, glossary, contents pages, pictures and check which of these features are found here and how they are used.

Reading and responding

- Demonstrate reading pp2–5 and model making simple notes. Explain to children that their notes must be shorter than the original text and can include diagrams as a way of summarising the information.

- Ask children to read independently to p27 and make notes to report back to the group later.

- Listen to children as they read, prompting and praising where necessary.